the
STORY
of
GRANDMA

A QUESTION & ANSWER GUIDE TO

Grandma's Life, Lessons, and Legacy

VANESSA PARKS

ADAMS MEDIA
New York London Toronto Sydney New Delhi

Adams Media
An Imprint of Simon & Schuster, Inc.
100 Technology Center Drive
Stoughton, Massachusetts 02072

First Adams Media hardcover edition November 2021

ADAMS MEDIA and colophon are trademarks of Simon & Schuster.

For information about special discounts for bulk purchases, please contact Simon & Schuster Special Sales at 1-866-506-1949 or business@simonandschuster.com.

The Simon & Schuster Speakers Bureau can bring authors to your live event. For more information or to book an event contact the Simon & Schuster Speakers Bureau at 1-866-248-3049 or visit our website at www.simonspeakers.com.

Interior design by Priscilla Yuen
Interior images © 123RF/annaguz, Olga Ponomarchuk, zenina

Manufactured in China

10 9 8 7 6 5 4 3 2 1

Library of Congress Cataloging-in-Publication Data has been applied for.

ISBN 978-1-5072-1716-0

ACKNOWLEDGMENTS

I have fond memories of my grandmother singing the lullaby "Too-ra-loo-ra-loo-ral" in her lilting Irish brogue when I was growing up. She lived with us, and I also remember Nana uttering dire-sounding warnings like "Woe betide ye" and "The devil mend ye." My three siblings and I didn't know what she meant, exactly, and yet we knew exactly what she meant.

Her name was Margaret Culkin Casey, and she was about twenty when she boarded a ship to cross the Atlantic from Galway to Boston. What was she hoping to find? I'll never know, because, by the time she died when I was twenty-two, I didn't appreciate how much I would come to wonder about these things. Now I have so many questions. Here's to your story, Nana.

And to my husband Jim's grandmother, Josephine Pane Amorello. She died at age thirty-six, soon after giving birth to my father-in-law, her eleventh child. Josephine, you were remembered with love by the thirty-five grandchildren you never knew.

CONTENTS

INTRODUCTION

Hello there, Grandma...

*What do you see as the biggest differences between
your childhood and mine?*

What was my parent like as a child?

How do you compare being a grandmother to being a mother?

*How close were you to your own grandparents?
What were they like?*

If you're lucky enough to be close to your grandma, it surely ranks right up there as one of the most treasured relationships in your life. There's the unconditional love, the good advice, maybe a quirky personality trait or expression that—hands down—makes you happy each and every time you think of it. And grandparents can be such a great source of family history too. No genealogical site will tell you about the likes and dislikes of family members or how they spent their days as a child.

There's so much more to learn! And if you don't ask, you'll never know!

That's where *The Story of Grandma: A Question & Answer Guide to Grandma's Life, Lessons, and Legacy* comes in. The more than one hundred questions you'll find inside cover a variety of topics: her early years, parenting, relationships, likes and dislikes, pivotal moments, amusing anecdotes, and perhaps a tragic tale or two. In short, the stuff of which family stories are made. These stories will entertain you, ground you, nurture you, and remind you of where and how you fit in and belong.

If untold, family stories and histories are lost. You don't have an endless amount of time to ask these questions. And if you don't learn the answers, you'll always regret it. So get to it! While an heirloom like a wedding ring or painting can be enjoyed by just one person, family stories can be enjoyed and owned by all. Here's to *The Story of Grandma*, a treasure to be passed on for generations.

HOW TO USE THIS BOOK

Think of this book as a conversation between you and your grandmother. You could give Grandma the book and have her answer the questions, but a much better idea is to sit down with Grandma, Nana, or Bubbe and settle in for a grand conversation. Ask her the provided questions, but know that the best, fullest answers will come from follow-up questions.

The first chapter contains easy, basic questions about family background and favorite things, making it a great ice-breaker. Rather than run through all these questions at once, you may want to save a few for each sitting. And no, you won't get through all the questions in one sitting. It will take time. Which—yay!—means more time with Grandma.

Plan to meet when you'll both be relaxed and not rushed, in a comfortable place where you won't be interrupted but will be able to take breaks. Then plan to meet again. And maybe again. Don't keep all the fun for yourself. Siblings or cousins may want to share the experience of compiling *The Story of Grandma*, taking turns at different chapters.

There's space on the pages for written answers, which can be filled by either you or Grandma. That may seem like a quaint notion, but think how thrilled future generations will be to have this keepsake with your and Grandma's handwriting.

But you may also want to bring along your computer or a recording app—or both—to capture Grandma's responses, so you don't miss a moment. Keep in mind that you'll have to transcribe the recording later. (At the beginning of the recording, you may want to state the date and who's speaking. Try to eliminate any background noise.)

Some questions are meant to elicit longer answers than others. The follow-up questions will be essential for drawing out a full story. If Grandma seems stuck on a question, try rephrasing it so it isn't a superlative. For instance, if she can't quite come up with the worst this or the best that, ask her to think of "one of the best" or "one of the worst." Or you might coax an answer by offering what your answer would be.

But don't rush to fill a void of silence. Be patient. It will give Grandma time to ponder. Or perhaps prompt her to fill the silence. But if an answer isn't coming, move on. Come back to a question that requires ruminating; remember to come back to it—a third or fourth time, if necessary. And if she really just doesn't want to answer a given question, so be it. (Though you'll be left to wonder why!) Pay attention to how engaged your grandmother is in the process. Don't let a session last too long. And end each session with a tentative time for the next one.

You'll also find space to include photos of your grandmother and other important family pictures. Try to include at least one photograph from all stages of Grandma's life:

a baby picture, photos of her as a young child and teenager, a graduation or wedding photo, a photo of her with your parent, and definitely a current photo of her with you and any siblings or cousins.

When *The Story of Grandma* is complete, be sure to share it with younger family members. It will help them build an identity and feel even more connected to the people they love. Be sure to treat it as the treasure it is and keep it in a safe place. Remember, this journal isn't just for you; it's for your children and, someday, your grandchildren. But don't let it sit there gathering dust. Perhaps you can create a new family tradition of going through it each year on Grandma's birthday or Mother's Day, maybe while playing her favorite song or enjoying her favorite food. Because by then, you'll surely know what they are.

CHAPTER 1

Quick Questions about Grandma's Background and Favorite Things

We start with a bird's-eye view, where you get to take in an overview of Grandma's life and likes in tiny, bite-sized morsels. This chapter is a great way to start the conversation with Grandma, because these questions should be easy to answer. Subsequent chapters contain questions that may require more thought or be a bit more difficult to answer.

Accordingly, instead of going through all of the questions in this chapter in one sitting, we suggest that you run through just a few of them at first. Then, start each subsequent session with a few of these relatively effortless queries before moving on to the chapter at hand.

So flit from one branch to another as you learn about things like Grandma's favorite animal, her best birthday, and whether she was named for anyone. Sure, you may already know the answer to a given question—her ethnicity, for instance—but keep in mind that the goal is not just to get to know Grandma better, but also to chronicle her story for future generations. Starting here, you can leave a trail of bread crumbs for a future great- or great-great-grandchild to follow back to their roots.

Where and when were you born? Tell me your full name. Were you named for someone?

How old are you now, as we're going through these questions?

Name your siblings from oldest to youngest. Where were you in the birth order?

Let's construct your family tree. Name your parents, grandparents, and great-grandparents, and, if you know them, the dates they were born and died.

_____

_____

_____

_____

_____

_____

_____

_____

_____

_____

What's your ethnic background?

_____

_____

_____

_____

_____

_____

_____

Where did you go to school (elementary, high school, undergrad, postgrad, other)?

_____

_____

_____

_____

_____

_____

What are your children's names? Grandchildren's names?

_____

_____

_____

_____

_____

_____

_____

_____

_____

_____

_____

_____

Name your favorite movie and favorite actor.

What's your favorite food? What was it when you were a kid?

What's your favorite song? Can you sing a line or two?

Tell me your favorite color.

Your favorite animal?

What was your best birthday?

What's a sound that you love?

CHAPTER 2

Shared Roots: Grandma's Ancestry and Childhood

Just as the roots of a tree not only anchor it but nourish it, a grandmother can be a wonderfully stabilizing and nurturing force in a family. And knowing about the roots of your family tree can provide that same kind of sustenance.

The questions in this chapter touch upon things like where Grandma grew up, her friends, and how she enjoyed spending time as a child. Maybe you've never given any thought to what Grandma was like as a little girl or a teen, but wouldn't you love to know? Was she shy? Vivacious? This is a good time to ask Grandma to pull out some photographs from her younger years. The photos might jog some memories or help spark conversation.

These Shared Roots questions also explore her relationships with her parents, siblings, and other meaningful people in her life. It may surprise you to hear how her best friend would describe her. Other questions in this chapter will delve a little deeper. Come take a closer look at what Grandma's childhood was like, and discover the experiences that helped shape the woman she is today.

What do you remember most about the place where you grew up? Tell me about the house and your bedroom. What feelings does it evoke when you recall it?

What was your favorite childhood game or way to spend time?

Who was your best friend as a child? What was he or she like?
What's one word he or she might use to describe you as a kid?
When was the last time you were in touch?

How would you describe your parents? Did you get along well with them? How did this evolve as you got older? Were you closer to your mother or your father? Do you think relationships between parents and children have changed since then?

Can you share a family story that your family used to tell when you were young? Would you ask them to tell it or would they bring it up on their own? What did you enjoy about this piece of family lore? What did you learn from it?

Did you have a happy childhood? Why or why not? What would you change about it today, if you could? Did this influence how you raised your own children?

What did you call each of your grandparents? Did you see them often? What was your favorite thing to do with them? In what ways has being a grandparent changed since then?

What do you see as the biggest differences between your childhood and mine? Which differences do you think are bad, and which do you think are good?

What kind of child were you: well behaved or rebellious?

What types of food did you eat growing up? Are there any foods that people just don't eat anymore? What about a favorite candy that's no longer available?

Who was your favorite relative growing up? Why?

What did you want to be when you were growing up?

What year of adolescence did you most enjoy? Least enjoy? In what ways is adolescence different today? In what ways is it the same?

Would you say you were confident or awkward? What were your insecurities? Did you eventually get over them? When? What helped you get over them, or prevented you from doing so?

Tell me about the people or events that had a significant impact—good and bad—on you. Have you thanked or confronted the people involved? Why or why not? Were people less expressive of their emotions when you were younger? Were they less likely to confront others?

CHAPTER 3

Branching Out: Romance and Other New Experiences

As Grandma became a teenager and young adult, it was time to branch out. There was a whole world out there to discover and explore, a world with things like dating, falling in love, and becoming independent. With no dating websites and apps, nor the ability to ask someone out via text, dating was different back in Grandma's day—and here you'll find out all about it.

It may be hard to imagine Grandma as a flirtatious young belle or as a giddy lovesick girl. But pursuing love and being in love is yet another dimension of her personality. This may not be the kind of thing Grandma typically opens up about, so here's your chance to pry without seeming as though you're prying.

Where did she and her spouse go on their first date? What was her first impression? Did she ever love anyone else romantically?

Though they definitely rank right up there, love and romance aren't the only new adventures for a young person making the leap from adolescence to adulthood. There's also leaving the nest, buying a first car, and having a drink. Find a place to perch and settle in as you explore this offshoot of Grandma's life.

How old were you when you had your first kiss? Did you do it out of curiosity or desire? Whom was it with? Was there a second kiss? Do you think kissing was a bigger deal when you were young than it is now?

Do you believe in love at first sight?

What was the craziest thing you did with your friends in high school? Would you do it again if you could? Did you all talk about it much as the years went by?

Do you remember the first time you got a little tipsy? How about a time you definitely got too tipsy? Tell me how old you were, whom you were with, and where you were.

What was the make and color of your first car? How much did it cost, and how did you pay for it?

How old were you when you moved out of your parents' home?
Where did you move? What cities or towns have you lived in?

What was the first thing you learned to cook or bake? Who taught you? Do you still make it today? Will you teach me?

Do you remember the first time you saw Grandpa (or your spouse/
partner) and what your impression was? How did you meet? What
did you do on your first date? Did you have to ask your parents'
permission? What attracted you to him/her? Did you ever love
anyone other than Grandpa (or your spouse/partner)?

Did Grandpa (or your spouse/partner) have a pet name for you?
Did you have one for them?

Tell me how Grandpa (or your spouse/partner) proposed. How long was the engagement? Were you nervous on your wedding day? How old were both of you? What did your dress look like? Who was in the bridal party? Tell me about the wedding and reception. How many guests were there? Did you enjoy it?

Tell me about something adventurous you've done. Were you nervous or excited or both? Did you ever do it again? Would you like to do it again? How would you feel if I did it?

Do you think it's okay to keep secrets from your spouse?

What advice do you have for me about dating? Do you think it's a good idea to date a lot of people? What are your feelings about people being more open about sex and sexuality nowadays? Do you have any words of wisdom to share with me about marriage?

Tell me about a time that you had your heart broken. How long did it take to get over it? Do you ever think about that person? Did you break someone else's heart? What about other types of heartbreak?

What's the most romantic thing Grandpa (or your spouse/partner) ever did?

CHAPTER 4

Rings of the Trunk: What Makes Grandma Grandma

If you examine photos of the rings of trees, you'll notice how different they are from one another, and yet how beautiful each one is. A tree's rings reveal not just its age but also what the weather was like during its life. In stressful times, a tree might not grow at all—unlike Grandma, who, we're sure, learned and grew from trying experiences. This chapter explores the life experiences that helped Grandma develop the qualities that define her—the rings of her trunk, if you will.

The questions in this chapter probably aren't ones to which you know the answers. And they may not be questions that Grandma has actively contemplated. This, then, may be one of those chapters that requires more time. Look back at those interviewing techniques suggested in the How to Use This Book section. For example, try to be comfortable with silence while Grandma contemplates an answer, and don't rush to fill the void. Maybe you can prompt a response by suggesting what your answer might be.

Grandma's responses will offer a glimpse into the life experiences that helped her earn any lines and creases on her lovely face, and will help deepen your understanding of what makes Grandma Grandma.

What age do you feel you are (that is, your subjective age versus your actual age)? Has this always been the age you've felt you are, more or less?

What are you most proud of in your life, and why? What's something you're not so proud of, and why? Have the types of things that make you proud changed as you've gone through life? What's the proudest moment you've had as a mother? As a grandmother?

Which of your senses would you most hate to lose: sight or hearing?
Taste or smell or touch?

Have you cried recently? Why? What about a good laugh?

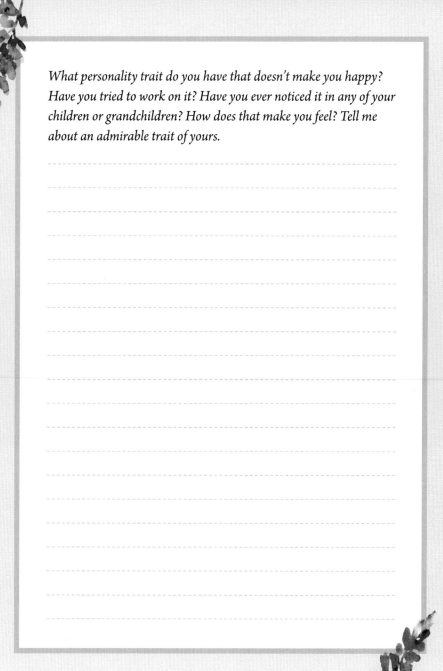

What personality trait do you have that doesn't make you happy? Have you tried to work on it? Have you ever noticed it in any of your children or grandchildren? How does that make you feel? Tell me about an admirable trait of yours.

What's your greatest fear? Have you ever had to face it? Do you have any lesser fears or phobias, like a fear of public speaking or a fear of snakes?

Are you a better talker or a better listener? Has this always been the case?

In what moments are you most content? What is it about these moments that gives you a sense of inner peace? Do you experience them often enough?

Do you have any advice you can share with me about pulling yourself out of a bad mood?

Tell me something about yourself that would surprise me or that no one knows. Do you intentionally not talk about this, or has it just never come up?

Are you a trusting or distrustful person? What events in your life helped foster this? Do you wish that you were more trusting or less so?

Imagine you were in a difficult situation, like stranded on an island or taken hostage. What qualities would you rely on to survive?

Do you think you had a defining moment in your lifetime? What was it?

What's the most challenging mental or physical health issue you've had to deal with? At what point in your life did you have to deal with this? What was challenging about it? Is there anything you'd handle differently if you could do it over?

CHAPTER 5

Bearing Fruit: Pregnancy, Motherhood, and Family Life

Your grandma is lucky enough to have seen her babies grow up and have their own babies. That certainly must rank right up there as one of the most joyful experiences of her life. There's the happiness for her children, and the happiness for herself. This chapter explores Grandma's thoughts on being a mother and grandmother, and her relationships with her own parents and family.

Good mothers and good grandmothers share many qualities, such as unconditional love and patience. But make no mistake: The two roles are different. Grandmothers have the benefit of having parented already and having learned from past mistakes. And, in fairness to moms in the thick of it, it's probably easier for grandmothers to be patient.

Being a parent is hard. Being a grandparent is liberating. Asking Grandma about the differences between the two will be fun. What would she do differently with her own children? What's her favorite way to spend time with you and any other grandkids?

And because she is your parent's parent, Grandma may be able to offer some invaluable (or delicious) insights into what your mom or dad was like as a child. What's the worst trouble they got into as a kid? Let's find out.

What do you think is the biggest difference between being a mother and being a grandmother? Which role have you enjoyed more? Which is more fulfilling?

What most surprised you about becoming a mother? What most
surprised you about becoming a grandmother?

What's the most significant change in parenting that you've seen in your lifetime? Do you think it's been for the better? Why or why not?

Which of your children was most rebellious? Which was most adventurous? Most obedient? If you could go back in time and react to their personalities and foibles differently, would you?

Did you want to be the same kind of mother that your mother was? In what ways? What did you want to do differently? How is your relationship with me different from your relationship with your grandmother(s)?

What was one of your favorite moments as a parent? What was one of your worst? What about your favorite and worst moments as a grandmother?

What's your best-loved way to spend time with your grandchildren?
Do you see us as much as you'd like?

What's the most trouble my parent got into growing up? How did you react?

What's your favorite family tradition? Why? What were some family traditions that you had growing up?

What is your wish for me and your other grandchildren? What had you wished for for your children as they were growing up?

If you hadn't had children, how would your life be different? If you could go back in time, would you have more children or fewer children?

What's a piece of advice you would offer a new mom? How about a new grandma?

CHAPTER 6

Feather the Nest: Fun and Frivolous Musings

Going through the questions in this chapter should be as easy breezy and entertaining as grabbing an old tire and swinging from a branch of the family tree. Things get light and fun as we explore some less serious topics. And while, yes, you really want to know some of Grandma's deepest thoughts and most sage advice, we think you'll both enjoy a bit of frivolity.

After all, the light side is part of her personality too. You'll definitely want to know, and be able to share, stories and factoids that make you giggle. Here you'll learn the kinds of things Grandma's girlfriends might have known about her, but your mom or dad might not. Things like the most repulsive thing she's ever eaten, or the worst fashion mistake she's ever made.

You may also find that Grandma, like many women, can be—or perhaps used to be—quite critical of her own appearance. Does she color her hair? When did she start? How does she feel about aging? Does she think any of her grandchildren look like her?

Or perhaps you're curious to know what she thinks about current fashions. Baggy pants? Thick eyebrows? Dish, Grandma. It's time to frolic!

What do you consider your best physical feature? Did you always feel this way? Is there anything you wish you could change about your appearance? Have you ever changed anything about your appearance? Are you more or less critical of your looks now, as compared to when you were younger?

What was your worst look in terms of fashion? What about your worst hairstyle or makeup choice? How long did you embrace it? How old were you?

What's a favorite piece of clothing that you've owned? How did you feel wearing it? What about favorite shoes?

What fashion trend have you seen in recent years that you just don't get (for instance, baggy pants, thick eyebrows, tattoos, or certain haircuts)? What decade do you think had the best fashions?

When did you start coloring your hair, and why? Did you stop? Or, if you've never colored your hair, why not?

What's the most repulsive thing you've ever drank or eaten? Tell me about the circumstances.

Do you remember the first time that something made you feel old, like noticing how young a police officer or physician looked? What makes you feel old now? Do you mind being old or do you embrace it?

How do you feel about getting older... the good, the bad, and the ugly? What makes you feel young? Which is preferable: being old or being young? Why?

Do you think that any of your grandchildren look like you or Grandpa (or your spouse/partner)? Do any of us remind you of yourself or other family members in different ways?

What's something sentimental that you bought for yourself, and when did you buy it? Did you have to talk yourself into it or was it an impulse? Do you still own it? If so, does it give you a bit of joy?

Do you have a favorite word? Do you like the sound of it or its meaning? Is there a word you can never pronounce correctly, or one that irritates you to hear mispronounced or misused?

Did you dance to a song at your wedding? How do you feel when you hear that song today? Can you sing a few lines?

Tell me about a time that you judged a book by its cover and were completely wrong. Do you think it's sometimes possible to accurately judge someone by their looks? Do we as a society put more or less emphasis on looks today than when you were younger, or is it about the same?

If you had to choose between movies, music, or books for the rest of your life, which would you go with, and why?

CHAPTER 7

Out on a Limb: School, Work, and Life Lessons

How much do you know about Grandma's life outside of her role as your grandmother? Perhaps not much. And that's just fine. After all, her most important role when she's with you is simply being your grandma. But it would be nice to get a glimpse of Grandma as a person separate from that.

In this chapter, you'll have the chance to explore the years during which Grandma progressed from a sapling to the source of strength that she is today. Before you came along, she spent years as a student, raising her family, and working either in the home or outside of it, or both. Knowing what those years were like is yet another way to have a better, more complete idea of who Grandma is.

Did she like school? What was her favorite job? Is there something new she'd like to learn? (A gift certificate to pursue this interest could be your next present to her!) Does her crowning achievement have to do with being a parent or grandparent or something entirely different?

Let's learn about Grandma's school days and her days as a student of life.

Did you enjoy school? Why or why not? What kind of student were you? What was your favorite subject? Did you speak up in class? Who was your favorite teacher, and why? What did you usually have for lunch?

What's something you've always wanted to learn but didn't (maybe something like learning another language, knitting, or making fresh pasta)? Why didn't you? Would you consider learning it now?

If you had been born at a later time or could choose another career, what do you see yourself doing? Why?

What was your first job, and how old were you? Did you enjoy it? What was your favorite job? Why? What did you learn from your least favorite job?

Share with me an important lesson you've learned in life. Why was this important? When did you learn it? Do you wish you'd learned it sooner?

Were you ever underestimated because you're a woman? How did you cope with that?

What was your favorite decade (that is, the 1950s, 1960s, and so on)? What did you enjoy about that period?

Tell me about an embarrassing moment you had in school. What about an embarrassing moment at work or just in general? Would you still be embarrassed if it happened today? What did you learn from these situations?

I'd like you to share some wisdom about friendship. What do you consider the most important quality in a friend? Do you think it's important to have close friends? Do you wish you had spent more time with friends or stayed in better touch over the years?

If one of your grandchildren had to endure a painful experience in order to learn an important lesson, would you try to save them from that pain?

What do you see as your greatest accomplishment? Was it difficult to accomplish? Why does it make you proud?

CHAPTER 8

Pruning and Regrowth: Things She'd Change and Things She Wouldn't

Trees are awe-inspiring, not just for their majestic strength, but also for the way they sway and even bend with the wind—which ultimately makes them hardier. As Grandma weathered storms throughout her life, there's a good chance she learned when to stand her ground and when to yield. But getting to such a place of profundity takes time and experience. Along the way, there certainly were missteps.

No one goes through life without regrets, nor should they. It's how you handle those regrets that's important. If you regret a disagreement that resulted in losing contact with a friend, you can make things right by rekindling the relationship. It's the mistakes that can't be undone that are harder to reconcile.

Knowing what Grandma might have done differently in her life—or what she wouldn't have—will offer insights into her temperament, her judgment, and her values. Some questions in this chapter are about regrets; others are about potential do-overs. As you hear what Grandma would and wouldn't change about her life, heed the lessons and let them influence the way you live your life.

Is there an invitation—maybe to a party, a date, or just for coffee— that you declined and regret? Why did you decline? Why do you regret it?

If you could pick a day to relive, which would it be? Is that because you'd want to enjoy it all over again or because you'd want to change it? If you'd want it to turn out differently, what would you do to change the outcome?

If you could live somewhere else, where would it be?

What's the most beautiful or memorable place you've visited? Have you been back? If you could travel anywhere tomorrow, where would you go? What was the worst vacation you went on?

Do any silly little regrets keep you up at night? What are they? When you look back over your life so far, do you see a common thread in regrets? Do they involve things you did or things you didn't do?

Looking back on trying times, how much of it turned out to really matter? Do you regret feeling stressed or unhappy over certain things?

What has been the most rewarding thing in your life?

Is there someone you should have apologized to but didn't? Why?
Do you have any advice for me on how to handle apologies?

What's the hardest thing you've ever had to do? Would you handle it differently today? In what way?

If you could pick just one thing to do differently or have one thing turn out differently in your life, what would it be?

Are you better at keeping secrets or telling them? Did you ever share someone's secret that you later regretted? Tell me about it.

What's the worst betrayal you've experienced? Have you forgiven the person who betrayed you?

Of all the technological advancements you've seen in your lifetime, from TV to computers to cell phones, which do you consider most helpful? Which do you think have been harmful? What's a technology that you used as a child that isn't around today?

Is there something about your life that you never would have expected?

CHAPTER 9

View from the Top: Looking Back, Looking Ahead, and Final Thoughts

We've come to the end of *The Story of Grandma*, but not the end of your grandma's story. It may be that this exercise leads to new growth in your relationship with Grandma. You may start to wonder about other aspects of her life and your family tree, and perhaps feel more comfortable or motivated to ask those questions.

In this final chapter, we pose some difficult questions. Death is an inevitable part of life, but conversations about it aren't. Yet knowing how Grandma feels about death and dying may make it easier for both of you when that time eventually—inevitably—comes. Does she believe in an afterlife? Is she afraid to die?

Not all the questions in this chapter are that heavy. Some give Grandma the opportunity to reflect on memorable moments, like the time someone gave her a really nice compliment. Or the chance to remember and talk about someone who's had an impact on her life.

This chapter offers up an assortment of existential questions about life and death, and also gives Grandma the chance to ask a question or two of her own. So go ahead: Climb to the top of the tree and take it all in.

How do you want to be remembered? Is that how you think you'll be remembered? Have you spent much time thinking about your legacy?

Grandma, is there something you'd like to ask me about myself? (Write down what her question is, and write your answer here, as well as Grandma's reaction.)

What are your views on religion and/or spirituality? How have these views changed from when you were younger?

How have your political views evolved? Who was the first president you voted for? Who was your favorite president? What historically significant events have you experienced, and how did they impact you?

Can you tell me about a time when you struggled to accept something? How long did it take you to accept the situation? What did this teach you about acceptance going forward?

Of all the societal changes that have occurred over the course of your life, which were the most unexpected or surprising? Which do you think have been the most positive?

Tell me about a time when someone was kind to you, whether it was a simple gesture or incredibly generous.

What's the nicest compliment you ever received? Why were you touched by it?

What person has been most influential in your life? Tell me more about this person. In what specific ways did he or she influence you?

If you could plan your last meal, what would it be?

What do you believe happens after you die? Do you think about your death? Are you afraid to die?

If you could learn exactly when and how you were going to die, would you want to know? Why or why not?

What did you think of going through these questions?

Is there anything I didn't ask you that I should have?

AFTERWORD

The Story of Grandma is done but not over. We hope you'll refer to this keepsake again and again, to remember Grandma and relive these memories. You can use this additional space in several ways. Grandma and anyone who participated in asking the questions should sign and date here. Again, think of future generations and what a treasure this will be for them. You've already asked Grandma what it was like going through these questions; perhaps you can record your own thoughts on the process. If some memory or anecdote occurs to you or Grandma later, jot it down here. Fill this space whenever you choose—soon after finishing the journey, or perhaps after Grandma passes.

NOTES

Photo ALBUM

Use the next few pages to affix some of your favorite photos. Be sure to include at least one photograph from all phases of Grandma's life: a baby picture, photos of her as a young child and teenager, school photos, a graduation photo, or a wedding photo. Include pictures from holidays and seminal family events: a baptism, bat mitzvah, adoption ceremony, quinceañera, breaking the fast on Eid al-Fitr, or celebrating Christmas or Diwali. You might even include a treasured recipe. Don't forget to select a few photos that capture the essence of Grandma, or that simply make you smile. And, of course, a photo of Grandma with her beloved grandchildren.

MOM–
Like You've Never Seen Her...

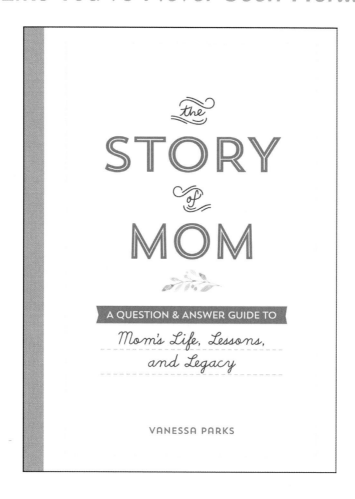

Pick Up or Download Your Copy Today!